Being ...

Famous Ones

Jeni Williams teaches literature and creative writing at Trinity University College, Carmarthen. In addition to writing poetry, she is a cultural critic writing on a wide range of subjects from dialectology to contemporary art. Her published work includes *Sideways Glances*, a groundbreaking book on Welsh art. She was the contributing editor of *Fragments from the Dark: Women Writing Home and Self in Wales*.

Being the Famous Ones

Jeni Williams

Parthian
The Old Surgery
Napier Street
Cardigan
SA43 1ED

www.parthianbooks.co.uk

First published in 2009
© Jeni Williams 2009
All Rights Reserved

ISBN 978-1-905762-44-6

Editor: Landeg White

Cover painting © Joe Avery/Glyndwr University
Cover design by Marc Jennings

The sketches of the author on the interior cover are by
painter and printmaker William Brown, the watercolour
is by portraitist Gordon Stuart.

Inner design and typesetting by www.lloydrobson.com
Printed and bound by Dinefwr Press, Llandybïe, Wales

Published with the financial support of the Welsh Books
Council

British Library Cataloguing in Publication Data
A cataloguing record for this book is available from the
British Library

Contents

After the Gas

for Mohammed Azdheh

After many days they were very hungry,
the men in uniform bewildered by the mountain and the empty villages.
There was a little rice and nothing else.
The snow was very thick and they shivered.
They were afraid of wolves.

When they looked up there were more mountains stretching up,
snow and behind the grey rock, grey sky.
The major said, we cannot live like this.
It is impossible.

So they took their guns and rope, went to the mountain, hoping
for something, anything, for they had eaten only rice.
They were afraid of the empty village,
of the dead child over his dish of dust,
of his dead mother with no eyes.

Their boots were wet and cutting their feet.
Many of them were come from the city.
They were afraid and hungry, falling asleep on the watch,
hands cramped and frozen on the trigger,
jerking awake with grey shadows stalking the trees.

In the dream light of dawn one or another cried out,
fearful and hungry.
There was a little rice and nothing else.
The major said, it is impossible:
we cannot live like this.

Some said the chemicals are everywhere,
even the snow is poisoned.
Some said if we shoot an animal the flesh will be unclean.
But the major said, there is only rice and snow.

On the mountain they found the cow,
thin and frightened, her owner disappeared.
Some said, he is dead surely, the chemicals are everywhere.
He may be dying in the city, some said.

We cannot shoot the cow, she is full of bad blood.
They forced her sideways down,
she was bellowing in fear,
tied her feet together, forced her to the ground.

She could not get up, they held her down, shouting.
Someone got a knife and sawed her throat open.
Then the colour melted the filthy snow.
Men gathered to warm their hands.

The smell of cooking drew them close.
They forgot about chemicals, about halal.
The smell of meat in the cold air,
even the smell warmed them.

When they looked up there were more mountains stretching up,
snow and behind the grey rock, grey sky.
There was a little rice and nothing else.
The major said we cannot live like this.

It is impossible.

Edges

There down the road yellow with late sun,
the girl in pink trousers is getting smaller,
skipping seriously, leaning forward,
precise, earnest, in her stripy top,
shiny hair stuck behind sticky out ears,
skin stippled with gold.

Dusk settles and the caws start up restless.
The sky is suddenly far away.
Where the field were, where the cows licked up grass,
new plots are marked out, the street is suddenly near,
the neat white houses fenced off,
their black rails twist up spiked with gold.

Red berries round the school yard,
blood red against spikes of green.
The calm night draws in.
The cars slow by the houses, past the girl.
One by one, all along the street, the lamps glow
first orange, then yellow, then gold.

The Grandmother

The grandmother was small and had many cats
                    and she lived alone on a small farm.
She was pretty, with black plaits to her waist.
Her name was 'flower full of raindrops'.

The old barn was full of sweet smells.
The grapes dried on thin lines in the comfortable dark
and the grandmother gave her grandchildren warm green raisons.
The small boy kissed her and asked,
'Nana, who coloured them so green?'
His grandmother laughed and said, 'it is magic.'
He stood in the barn and thought about this hard.

Every New Year, the grandmother painted eggs blue and yellow and red.
The small boy hugged her and asked,
'Nana, how did you colour the eggs?'
His grandmother laughed and said
'I ask the chickens to make them like that for my grandchildren'.
He watched the big brown chickens scratching
and talking to each other in the yard and wondered.

Sometimes the small boy worried about things.
He asked, 'Nana, are you not scared in this big house alone?'
And his grandmother kissed him and laughed
and said 'No, I always fly.
Someone throws a rope into my garden
and I catch the rope with my cats
and we travel up into the sky and far away.'

And the small boy thought how nice this was:
to catch a rope and fly up into the sky and far away.
He wondered how the cats could catch the rope
but he never asked his grandmother.
He stroked the cats and looked at their secret eyes,
stroked their soft fur and thought that, maybe,
they can.

Being God

He wants to drive her mad:
a strange ambition perhaps,
though not unusual in a certain kind of man.
He did, after all, succeed once before.

It was a thrill.
He liked the control it gave him,
just as he likes to capture images on film
and lock them away.

The other woman tried to kill him – or herself –
it hardly matters which since
neither attempt was serious.
She wept.
He took her to hospital.

He was so innocent,
so much in love.
He was both innocent and loving:
it was all
her fault.
She was mad.

Now he needs someone else
to play small and vicious games with,
to love, to spurn, to love,
to turn her head.

Such a thrill.
He's a big man.
He likes flying too.
Looking down.

In memoriam Kalan Kawa Karim

Murdered, Swansea, 6th September 2004

A fine day for the march. The curious
watched from doorways then walked off to unknown
busy lives, bored with chant and furious
protest. But, by the roadside and alone

for the quiet minute's length, an old man
slowly uncovered his head. He looked down,
acknowledging the brief and shattered span
of a good life, then left. No speech in town

denouncing such purposeless violence,
moved me so much as that man standing there,
head bent, holding his cap, the small silence
growing all round us. We walked to the square

and the cars, which had paused for the event,
moved on into a new, sunlit moment.

Earning their Keep

There they are, my small chickens,
rocking in the wild high trees,
my bright white and black speckleds.
There – and they won't go to bed.

Better to annoy neighbours,
shriek in the deep black of night,
dig to Australia, their
big, dirty toes busy in

my flowers, shout at the cat,
or the squirrels, cock their heads,
mutter to themselves, surprised,
or alarmed, at everything.

They uncover every bulb,
skitter on the kitchen roof,
crow with screwed up eyes, puffed chest,
tongue sticking out with effort,

astonished every time, and
pleased, with the huge noise they make
which daily follows me past
the smiling Turkish tailor.

Now, finally, this morning,
rolling off a cushion in
the dark quiet of the shed,
the density of white stone:

the perfection of an egg.

Framing

The café is in Spain.
Early summer,
the brown blind half-way down the window-frame.

Outside the roof garden is full of sun,
old elegance and a palm tree:
a square edged by green spikes.

The window frames a young man hunched in a blue shirt and tie,
frames his laptop, his beer,
the white haze of his cigarette.

He is developing a double chin.
His hands are cramped; yet, leaning forward,
almost loving, his fingers flick and slide over the keys.

Air slowly drifts through the lozenge of window,
pale lights hang over the bar.
soft, washed colours.

Elsewhere I watch the play of hands:
here, gently resting on a waist, there
on a shoulder. An arm stretches out then falls.

The fans turn slowly.
Dark beams, marble floors.
Jasmine like sunlight filtered by the blinds.

Three thin women sit together:
one touches her hips,
another closes her arms over her chest.

She holds herself a moment, rocks,
then, as the moment rushes on
fingers her red lips.

No clutter here.
Emotions leap in sparks
through empty space.

Photographs of old men turn towards us from three scuffed walls,
light calm on their lined faces, their dusty suits.
Black and white images with black intense eyes.

On the fourth wall, a woman. Naked.
She lies with her back to me,
the delicious curve of hip and buttock sketched in charcoal,

Her head
carefully placed
outside the frame.

Stone

That lump of stone got me today.
Old red sandstone stuck fast,
choking the roots of a tree.
Then the sea tore them out and cast them here
coughed into sand, half buried.

What I see here is the enormity of fact.
The stone chokes the twisted tree
and the tree cannot claw the stone from its craw.
The sea has thrust them far from home,
the stone weights the root and pulls it down, under.

But the human heart does not brood on gravity,
the eye is in love with change, the unfinished evolving human face.
See how the sandstone head heaves up
towards us, rough mouth open, holes for eyes.
These miracles happen in the beating heart.

Crocodile Songs

(i)
Underwater, trembling,
I caress those dangling thighs.
It is the waiting that's the most delicious.

I press my aching teeth through a
warm and fragrant softness.
The juice spurts with a shriek.

(ii)
Early summer and Icarus hung in the blue air
amongst tendrils of cloud he drifted
in the perfumed air over valleys
purple with buddleia...

Clouds and sky? life isn't like that.
How could the boy think, with such
weightless feathery legs, he could escape
my desire, my corkscrew clamp, my gullet?

As I brighten I sing to the imperious sun.
We are the elemental powers, we work together.
The clouds disappear, the perfume thickens:
it gets hard for the boy to breath.

Between us we have him,
fire and water in a pincer feeding my open jaws.
Golden Icarus slips and a feathered snack
momentarily warms my cold belly.

(iii)
I adorn myself with water lilies.
Unobserved logman.
Honeysuckle sweetens the steam rising from my pool.

(iv)
There was a moment, long ago,
when I was still, quietly flexing my tail
in a perfect world, the sky a shell over me
and the soft rocking dark.

But then I could not sleep anymore.
It grew hot. A water rat twisted in my belly.
I reared my ravenous snout and the sky tore.
I blinked and was born to this warm spiced slime.

Diary of a Mistress

Today I looked out of the window and thought of you.
I am going grey now, bones going brittle like a bird's.

Today the wind broke the clouds, rain fell:
the pond clogged with elder leaves then overfilled.
Last week I pulled a bloated frog out of water
squirming with tadpoles – black stomachs with tails –
ravenous mouths tearing, twisting into rotten flesh,
I tossed it under the elder tree. Buried it.

I muse at the wind ruffling the fennel,
soft, feathery, delicate, at the smell coming off it.

I think of it touching my skin.
Such a strong clear green.

Welsh Towns beginning with F

(i)   Felin-foel
How can a mill be bald?
I think of it there, waving its bare arms,
standing drunk and hairless on a hill.

(ii)   Ferryside
Ferryside could be a place to end your days,
perhaps with a jewelled brush and pan.
A jewelled sweeping brush: I'd like that.

(iii)   Ffestiniog
Ancient warriors lose themselves in Ffestiniog.
It's not just the crazy slate sculptures,
the wan wraiths are bewildered by tiny trains and tourists.
Their voices echo through the splintered stones:
A fair day for fighting when we've fasted.
Ah to be feasting at Ffestiniog in the faint, the far-off future...

(iv)   Fforestfach
Once I was frantic in Fforestfach:
A small place but I couldn't see the wood for the trees.

(v)   Flint
Rough, a tough town.
If you go there
strike a light.

(vi)   Fishguard
People are always telling me that Fishguard is a great place.
Not anyone who was my friend.
No-one I would trust.

(vii)   Fron-goch
What's in a name? Once
there was Welsh whisky here, long ago,
then prisoners jabbering in German
and Irishmen after the Easter Rising,
mocked by false spirits and failure.
All those histories hidden at Fron-goch,
a smooth rosy breast of a place.

Giving

(i)

It was himself he gave away, the old man,
discovering flowers, ribboned, wrapped,
abandoned on a dusty evening
in a Liverpool phone box that late August.

He ran, lit with glad extravagance.
Fragments of a love story, long gone, resurfaced
when he thrust them in a stranger's astonished arms:
a fragrant gift.

From his fractious memories
he faltered a line from Shakespeare,
then stumbled away
into the distant, the widening dark.

(ii)

Discovering flowers, ribboned, wrapped –
when he thrust them in a stranger's astonished arms
fragments of a love story, long gone, resurfaced.

It was himself he gave away, the old man:
he faltered a line from Shakespeare
in a Liverpool phone box that late August.

He ran, lit with glad extravagance,
then stumbled away
into the distant, the widening dark:

a fragrant gift,
from his fractious memories
abandoned on a dusty evening.

(iii)
Into the distant, the widening dark,
he ran, lit with glad extravagance,
discovering flowers, ribboned, wrapped,
abandoned on a dusty evening –

a fragrant gift
in a Liverpool phone box that late August –
fragments of a love story, long gone, resurfaced
from his fractious memories.

When he thrust them in a stranger's astonished arms
then stumbled away
and faltered a line from Shakespeare,
it was himself he gave away, the old man.

Killing a Pigeon

All I can say is that it is hard
to kill a pigeon
after waking in the middle of the night to
the cats tossing a terrified bird in the front room.

It hides under the sideboard, panting.
It should not be in this alien place,
obstacles everywhere and walls,
and two cats chattering with excitement.

Somewhere else, over the phone,
the problem of death –
of a pigeon's death –
seems amusing

but here it is quiet dark night
and in the living room
the cats play with
an injured bird.

It is in their nature to chatter their teeth,
to growl deep in their throats.
It is in the nature of the pigeon to flick its head,
eyes starting in shock.

Bloody feathers lie scattered on the white mat.
It is only a pigeon:
there are so many pigeons
and they are a nuisance.

Ah, but this is a single bird,
its heart thudding in my hand,
its body torn and trembling.

If it were a mouse
I could kill it quickly with a spade.
But it is too large.

I should kill it with a small sharp knife,
pressing the blade into living flesh
or slicing off its head in a quick jerk.

But I cannot do it.
The terrified creature pants
in my hand.

My grandfather drowned kittens.
I imagine its wings soggy and frantic in a bucket of water.
Its head ducking and straining under my hand.

It is the middle of the night and I cannot kill a pigeon.
Birds die under cars but I cannot
drive, deliberately, over a pigeon.

It should be easy to wring its neck
– just a twist of a wrist –
I try but it struggles away.

The pigeon huddles against the plant pots outside.
Half past one in the morning and a full moon
and I cannot kill a pigeon.

It drags itself across the acres of the small yard.
I think of slamming the kitchen door
on its neck but I know I cannot.

I tell myself it will get better and lock the door –
but I dream of war
and torture and frightened eyes and,

in the morning, it is still there,
clinging to a sliver of shelter by the bins,
lying on its back, gasping,

head snaking side to side,
eyes thickening,
flinching away.

Busy morning and
people eat breakfast next door,
drive past listening to music, to the news,
to each other, laughing on the phone.

Here the pigeon shudders in my palm.
Eyes glazing, it looks smaller now. It is dying.
The cats emerge blinking and puzzled.
It is in pain. I smash its head with a brick.

Referral to Medical Foundation

(i) Preliminaries

Please note:
that in order for the medical foundation concession
regarding accommodation in London
to operate
the applicant must show that she or he
    a) is a survivor of torture
    b) will need ongoing care or treatment
    c) needs the specialist services of the medical foundation

Please note:
    that the medical foundation
    does not operate
    access to family, community or other support
    which are available by other means.

Please note:
    That the medical foundation
    sees only the first 10 people on duty every day,
    Monday to Friday.

Note:
    Please fax this form to the medical foundation;
    please send a copy of the form to the applicant
    and to our duty case worker.

Note:
    Registration starts every day;
    At 12
    Noon.

Section B: history of torture

Duration:
Six days.

Nature of torture:
raped by soldiers;
several times;
repeated over two days;
shouting;
death threats;
put in cell.

Other experiences of organised violence:
saw her sister tortured (face burned in boiling water).

Current mental and physical health (in applicant's own words please):
finds it difficult to talk about effects;
has experienced nightmares.

Referrer's observations and concerns
None.

Once

There was a man who went fishing,
but the water went out and the fish with it
He caught a small orange crab –
kept it on a plate in the freezer,
alone, frosted with all the ice in the world.

There was a man once who played music and sang
of roses and eyes, of gardens and perfume.
The orange skies above Kuwait
put a stop to that.

There was a man who was once
the cleanest man in Iraq.

There was a man once who could dance
better than you ever saw,
waving a yellow handkerchief.

Once there was a man who had slept in the snow
and had forgotten how to be warm,
forgotten how to breathe in a room,
how to be safe.

Puzzles

What did he say before he left?
The tall man with eyes who said so very little.
He tapped his fingers on the window.

She thinks he smoked but
it is difficult to work out
what she made up in the half-light.

It was hard to see,
a hot evening and, yes, it was, sweat in her eyes.
The tall man tapped his cigarettes, wiped his lips.

The angry voices bit her face, like acid on skin.
Then her mother snapped the blinds.
Her father gazed at his feet.

Tonight she is frightened, sick,
her thin body with its scrub of hair,
rolls across the silent acres of her narrow bed.

Her clenched father, his small neat feet.
Her mother's smooth back as she reached up
and pulled down, pulled down with a dark ripple of hair.

In the shuttered room with its slats of dust
the chalk screech of a cricket jumps on the edge of her skin,
her eyes prickling, hot and wet.

A loud sound downstairs.
Then something soft.
Falling.

Outside her dark window,
cats arrange themselves in sequence,
patterns zigzagging the streets.

Her father hunched, looking down.
Her mother against the blinds.
Something soft. Falling.

Her stomach hurts.
Twisted in her familiar bed,
she strains to the silence of the strange downstairs.

The Brilliance of Stained Glass

for Euros Childs

So with a shiver at the edge of vision
he opened his eyes to extraordinary things:
simple stories in rhyme, blueberries, ice cream,
crickets in the marran grass, sea holly,
the lazy wash of the Pembrokeshire summer sea.

Still bright after thirty years,
singing, humming in the dark,
indomitable, shaking his head.
The sky lights up with cartoon sea gulls,
luminous beings float in starry air.

His fingers sprout feathers,
gleam waxen and gold.

Learning

The small bird fits snugly into the boy's
pocket, his heart contracting tenderly.
It was abandoned, he thinks, this vivid
cheeping thing he's rescued from the hedgerow.

It was alone: no mother, no father.
He walks slowly in his new uniform.
Careful. The grey shorts rub against pink legs
unused to the English cold. The Master

makes loud jokes; the boys in a crocodile
of quiet order. The hedgerows are full
of green smells and birdsong and spring flowers.
He wants to stop, stroke the soft faces of

violets in the grass. He likes tiny things
the best. He is serious, open-eyed,
learning new names, new things: he's heard that if
you pick cow parsley your mother will die.

Sometimes the boys hold hands, by accident,
before they remember not to. He is
seven now and holds the small bright bird safe.
Its yellow beak gapes wide. He strokes its head.

He wonders at its huge eyes, soft speckled
feathers, its bones like brittle ice. He wants
to give it worms, wants it to hop onto
his hand and sing. It cheeps insistently,
urgently. He does not know it will die.

Daisies

She had forgotten she was unique
with all the things rushing past her,
the shopping, cleaning
and television a coloured backdrop
to a life sliding past too fast.

She had forgotten to praise the matchless ocean,
though she lived near the sea
and the sand beckoned daily, enticing
with its salty driftwood, its plastic bottles of stories
from somewhere else. Had forgotten that
the extremities of the body define its delicacy:
wrists, ankles – sticks that break too easily.
There had been too much forgetting.

The daisies had always been a nuisance, she thought,
but when she fell, that day, pegging washing,
and lay, in the crushed clover and the absence of birds,
she was astonished by strangeness.
Supine, she thought, *lupine, carnadine, multitudinous*
Incarnate, incandescent, compassionate. Improbable.
A childhood passion for Latin returned, surprising her heart.
She lay for a long time, disconnected, full of bright words.
The familiar rain started to speckle her wondering face.

Now she saw the daisies: soft-petalled, golden-eyed,
tilting-headed, pink-streaked, thin sappy-stemmed.
A multitude *but with no like or equal*,
and *pushing up, fresh as a*.
The fine hairs on their fleshy leaves beaded:
carnal, succulent. Latin again.

The eyes of the day closing now,
the sound of oceans pressing in her ears now.

She was *supine*. Certain of it now.
The luminous stars tumbled in her head,
the daisies little flashes of light now,
the rain thickening now,
the clothes sodden heavy on the line now –
though she didn't look anymore –
and she grew
colder
cold.

Being the Famous Ones

So, after all, somewhere it is true.
Desperate adventures do happen.
And the magical ones in their shorts and gym slips
finish their labours and stretch suntanned limbs
amongst picnics of cold ham, and checked tablecloths
with a dog, sometimes a monkey inexplicably acquired
from a musical foreigner bowing with gratitude.

After the edges of dangerous cliffs, rising sea water, echoing wells,
after the treachery of dark races and dirty hands,
. they rest amongst apple cores bitten down to the quick.
Blackbird and lark sing in equal measure,
the mayblossom floats lazily into their eyes –
for now it is a time of bright joy:
it is spring in their wholesome world.

Indeed this is how they live – the other half who are not me.
No money troubles can smudge the lines of their certainties.
Their days are decorated by the admiration of peasants.
Their parrots do not swear; their cats do not
have fleas.

On Travelling and Maps

It was, possibly, a mistake –
to travel so far, so fast –
although it remained an adventure,
it was on shaky foundations.

Yet he knew how to read maps, to admire clarity,
to seek only the distance between things; knew
how to forget the nervous intravenous insertion,
by razor or needle, of fire, to ignore
the churning rattle and whisper of the forest floor,
and the black insects, everywhere hysterical with dusk.

For how else to travel from one place to another?
How else to leave both behind?

As he drove, solid land slid into swamp,
abandoned histories resurrected themselves
in flashes on the glittering edges of vision.
His bloody thoughts surfaced to minefields.

He stumbled further, through dripping water
          and a nightfall of spiders
But his sense of gratitude for north and west
drew him onward through a partial paper world.
The words faded before they turned familiar.

In the bone-thin mountains he listened to the echo of his thoughts,
white paper slipping through rigid fingers.
He was tired, aching, bitten.
Yet, wet amongst the clouds,
he forgave the shortcomings of maps,
stared at the purple sky, at the starflowers
        opening in early morning frost,
the ice catching in his throat.
The birds stirred and sang Bartok.

Herons

I slow down,
sit with a milky coffee,
try not to listen to the old man
on the next table whose eyes jerk sideways,
having quiet arguments with himself
over his fried eggs.

By the station entrance opposite the café
a man waves his arms, shouting.
Almost an hour.
He was there as I left the station,
crossed the road, opened this door,
came in.
There now as I return.

I wanted to slow down
to cast my mind away

but the shabby man in the station
sweeps the litter with such a sorrowful air,
and on the seat opposite a thin man
in a thin coat stares at his thin black hands,
and useless pity wells up inside.

I saw snowdrops in my garden this morning,
thrust up through the nodules of moss,
their dense white and dark, spikey green
shining amongst blackened leaves and old geranium stems.

Last week the cliff slid into my garden:
everything smashed,
the chicken run splintered to firewood.
The chickens, puzzled and noisy,
scratch and peck at piles of soil and shale
search for grain in the rubble,
huge rust-orange lumps of rock split along flat planes.

Yet today the jasmine starts to flower,
bits of yellow in the mess of rock and snapped struts
and I am alive;
below the rocks the broken apple tree will pulse again
slowly white blossom and bright leaves will reappear.

I sit on the empty platform, waiting for the train
my bag is full of things to do,
books to read, reports to write.

Sunday emptiness.
As I write I watch my bangles slide over my wrist.

I want a thin stream of clear water,
I want starflowers in shadowed hollows
and the smell of fresh garlic,
I want the brilliance of fresh leaves as the new sun
pours through tender translucent green.

Round my feet hobbles a dirty pigeon,
the bunched claws of her twisted foot
throw her off balance.
She rolls with each strutting, staggering step,
head clacking back and forth like a mechanical bird.

Here is February.
Every year the February grey hangs on, unbearable
till, at the last moment, when
it feels impossible that things can ever change,
the smell of white jasmine will fill Hanover street.
And thin sunlight will lift the blinds.

What kind of self do you take on a journey?
On what kind of journey can you take yourself
on an empty grey Sunday?

It is happening now:
I am leaving, looking for spring.

The train runs close by the gleam of sea,
ruffled waves sliding over and
scattered rocks jut through.
Like silk it is.
Gleaming like metal,
like a skein of light.
The carriage is full of light and the smell of salt.
I am leaving the station far behind, the café and the sadness.

On an empty train
I take an empty self.
I am open to the hugeness.
of the sea by my side.

On the rocks
in that space, in that light,
I count eight herons.

Old Man Crocodile

Old man crocodile
lying on the surface, idle flicker.
Log man crocodile
with very few teeth.
He stinks of cigarettes.

Why would he slide under, slip under the cool water,
quietly snap the birds' forgetful feet?
Kindly old crocodile, stretching in the sun,
he would not pull the youngsters down
and into black water.
How cold it is down there.

When disappearances happen,
they are not his fault.
Logman floating though the river's scattered light.
Does he sing tonight, dreaming
happy long agoes and far aways, in story time?
Does he dream the sea and the fishes' spoiling flash?
Shattered light on the thick, muscular surge of green water,
it catches the sun, throws it up again in the air.

There is no end to his cold dream.
He is a miniature croc, sitting obedient.
He is suddenly grown: a sea crocodile, fifty feet or more,
snapping his jaws to the melody of delight,
the planets swim through crystal heavens as cold as his eye,
their sung spell tricks us, high sweet music winking
too far away to touch.

Old croc, brown lump on the surface
rotten teeth on display.
He floats sideways, circles and slips under.
There's a tug and a twist and down she goes.

Sickness

for Rosemary

I suppose it was the way he moved,
you said, wondering.

From a distance it was as if
he required a staff for those long walks
through great hills of sand amongst the mad crickets sawing,
the hot breath of the day scorching his neck.

But it was evening then
and you were standing outside
a Swansea post office.

That was when you saw him,
walking through rubbish and cars.
A crisp moment and you saw his elongated earlobes
swing in delicate scoops of flesh.

A rough staff, the extraordinary earlobes.
An intricate, coloured blanket.

He was tall
in a haze of yellow
sunlight smoothing the curve of
his smooth skin as he walked
past the Uplands bookshop.

As he walked he was
in another space,
in a suspended bubble,
in a gauze balloon of light.

He walked out of a dream,
he knew your name,
he shook your hand.

Close up he was different:
grey, thin, sick.
He was homeless, and in Swansea;
and you sickening for home.

Dark Heart

For the dark heart of this dark story builds
somewhere else, just
as a flash of light, as a building explodes,
as a wave curls up and over a sheet of newsprint,

as the high rise rises up and trembles,
as the great ship drowns under the rocking waves,
as the distant plane slides across a cardboard sky,
and drops small flashes through the sparkling air.

Now a young boy bites his lip.
His slim dark mother grips him tight.
They are leaving house and church and friends.
They are walking up into the night sky.

It is a furnace of sweat and fear.
The young woman holds his hand more tightly:
she thinks she will vomit.
Her mind is full of a thousand black things jumping.

Deep below its surface lie fingers
snapped like sugar canes,
lie stained rags, a rusted nail,
lie bones split and frosted with slug,
lies the taste and stink of damp, metallic as blood,
lie a thousand jumping things.

I look sideways at the stars,
think of a boy with curly hair and dimples,
of a slim dark woman with braids and smooth black eyes.

They are speaking
but so far away
I cannot hear them.

Their hands sketch absence.
Their voices drift thin, frightened,
scatter on the dark wind.

My heart is dead now.
I am sick and dead.
I stay at home in the dark.
I look at the dead, dead fire.

So a Poem is about You and not about Me

outside my window –
which is not your window though we could pretend –
the unconscious trees are shifting in scorching sunshine.
The sun is, in fact, orange.
An old woman in blue walks to her red car and drives off

and the intense young men clustered on the corner,
heads bent, pulsating with talk, drumbeats,
are all thin black arms, vivid, brilliant eyes.

Far

Now he exists only
in the movement crawling onwards,
he's lost himself, stares
at his brown cracked hands.

What to be frightened of now but himself?
Something inside his bones aches.
His arm reaches over his head,
pulls the dark blanket down.

Fear. I think it's in all of us.
Memories slide under the blanket,
the belly cramps with emptiness,
the hollow night expands.

He remembers he once threw yellow blossoms into the river,
that lilac and buddleia sweetened the birdsong once,
that once he walked under a hot sky
freckled with blue summer.

Across the street a thin girl is lost.
She walks into the wilderness of neon
where the women wander with no clothes,
their cadged cigarettes close against the winter sleet.

Measures

i.m. Ahmed Dadkhoo

Here life is concentrated in fine lines,
the measured breath, the deliberate hand
moving from heart to lip:
a dialogue of gesture, breath and sound.

The man with the broken heart moves slowly,
his eyes move slowly, his lips
open and close on perfection:
Hafiz, Sa'di, Rumi, Khayyam.

Their verse distills the living breath.
The old man smoothes the page he knows by heart –
faint marks of birds on sand.
The wind is blowing now, the sea coming in.

It is enough, finally, to share the measured breath of others,
to re-inscribe their patterned words,
to speak with, to find connections,
to hold fast the eye and heart.

All is refined now to line.
This is what lasts now: the rhythm of breath.
The loop of rhyme that binds,
holds firm against a coming silence.

Turning

What he wanted was medicine to heal the sadness.
But that December he could not leave the house.
The rooms were brittle with polished surfaces
and the spiders, spinning webs in sterile space,
caught nothing and starved.

In February he stared at the sheep in the sodden field
and the river pushing against its banks, gazed
at a small dog silhouetted against the rising water,
mused on duty and went out into the rain.
Returned to the dust free rooms and the boredom of Sundays.

Night after night through all that winter
the old man nursed his sadness,
struggled and sat in the quiet.
Then white April came with birdsong to let in light
and he and the world turned.

Chickens

Last night I watched reports from Afghanistan:
singing disallowed, a woman's finger chopped
like meat for painted nails, a man blows a woman's head off
in a stadium of men and boys eating popcorn.

Weeping hysterically an eleven year old seeks a divorce,
shows where her husband knifed her,
the bruises of his beatings, shows
the melted flesh on her legs where she set herself alight.

Today three children whisper in my garden.
One little girl, five years old,
determined, pale skin, dark eyes, neat short hair,
holds out her hand to the small chickens.

They quiver and stalk up and down on their muscular toes,
long necks stretched, eyes curious and surprised.
They like to sit on top of each other,
spreading their wings on the dirt in the sun.

The small girl squats quiet, composed.
Do you speak Pashtō? Dari? Uzbek? Tajik?
She shakes her head.
She sings to the chickens with bread in her hand.

Chickens: what I called my children when they were small.

Her fingernails shine with red and silver polish
The chickens dance closer,
Skitter away, return to the waiting hand.

safe in my chicken coop, a small bird sings in Pashto
sings to the small chickens.
Small bird with painted nails,
pale, luminous skin.

Underground

Sometimes
pregnant women eat coal.
The soft steam coal of Yorkshire bubbles
like black toffee with sticky tar.

Try it in secret, then open your mouth:
the electric flames will dance out,
blue, green.

Lick your nose pure as a bright new spring,
before a smear of soot settles over the shine.
It's a baptism of fire.

You may crave stronger stuff,
hunger for a deep world of
crooked corridors and flooded by-ways
alive and rattling with rats and black beetles.

The diamond delights of
Welsh anthracite lie deep
underground, out of reach.

Your teeth will crack if you weaken,
feed your black fantasies.
Turn your back on these dark hankerings.

Despite all, a small firm face will grow underground,
will surface, fingers, hair and skin like water,
nose as clean and sweet as new bread.

Astonishing, the soft touch of her lips,
her urgent imperious mouth,
her hungry astonishing eyes.

Reaching

This was my dream:
four figures coming out of the wood,
two women, a girl and a child.

From the road I could see the small white statue,
arms outstretched in blessing.

Close up, she was broken, blind, dirty:
green stains on the folds of her gown.
Her draped arms suspended,
the right hand fingers truncated,
the index finger of the left snapped off, hanging by a wire.

When they came out of the wood it was dark,
faces blued by the knife-cold.
For a long time they had walked in the scratchy shadows.

There was no sound on the hill.
The wind.
There was the wind I suppose.
But nothing more.

The walking was hard:
rough ground and stones.
When the rain started it was more difficult.
Stones with a film of grease and their feet
slid sideways unexpected.

Behind the women, the thin girl,
head bent with dirty hair,
swollen eyes, carrying a silent child.

I do not know where they came from.
They did not speak.
Their clothes were wet
and torn.

Behind them the wood reached forward.
The thick, reaching dark.

Interpreting the Ore Book

At first, the very thought of 'bedded
manganese deposits' suggests something dull, stilted,
rather like uncomfortable sleeping arrangements
amongst compacted bank accounts,
and possibly purple, though I'm unsure why.

But then, suddenly, I'm thinking of an Indian mongoose and,
before you know it, I'm onto pythons and Mowgli and wolves
and the British empire on which the sun never –

Even better, perhaps, than 'the alluvial
diamond deposits of the orange river'
which sounds so much more promising at the onset
but where the glittering scented elements sink,
on closer inspection, into the wavering sludge of an estuary.

On the other hand – like a forgotten place
behind the white flares lighting the motorway
and cars streaming through the night
from one built-up place to another –
'oil shales and tar sands' seems poetic
in a homely, Port Talbot, sort of way.

Chai

for Jasir Issa

'One day,' you said, mock seriously, bringing me a cup of chai,
'it will be too late. You will meet your Creator
and He will say, "I created sugar for the
pleasure of mankind, why did you reject my gift?"'

A lesson in sweetness. Milk and no sugar for me:
this marks a difference between worlds.
Spiced chai. All the foreign doctors in the world
sweeten it with the god's gift. Not us.

In the meeting house, I serve tea
to thin young men, lost, far from home.
Their anxious eyes register loneliness,
They ask for 4, 5, no, 6, spoons.

It is some kind of gift, after all, though not holy.
Razeh has not eaten for two days.
'Nice lady,' he says, bitterly,
'this life is shit.'

Bipolar

for Berthold

You're in love. He loves you.
Presents every day,
flowers, books.

The exact, perfect choice of wine,
chilled, delicious. And now
you're moving in with him.

He's captivating.
His hands describe eternity
and hold you together.

The skies expand to blue heavens.
The nightingale sings in the blue dusk.
Holidays in the sun. Plenitude.

Here is the famed happiness,
the golden times are here.
This could not, cannot, end in tears.

Then he's gone. Closed like a fish.
Flat-eyed, belly up.
This is how he sets you free.

You find it hard to breathe,
belly inside out, clenched round a grief.
A puff of words and then – like

a fall of yellow leaves patterning the river,
that's lit up in sunlight for a moment,
a moment of clarity, and then

undercurrents you can't see drag it sideways
into fragments – it's in decay and
disintegrates before your very eyes.

Now it's a shape, a ghost,
a story you tell yourself,
that you try to remember.

Ah, the mocking bird:
to be in love is
never enough.

Outside

A bicycle on a road,
a phone box by a field.
Rain.

The graceful tracery of cow parsley
flattens against the stained glass,
springs back.

The nettles lean in lush sharp clumps,
gust inwards, slip over wet panes.
The shape inside wavers.

Outside the water slides into black ridges:
a cobweb on the receiver,
a voice in her ear.

And suddenly hot mouths and tongues run
in scalding circles over her bare arms.
Her softest skin flinches, shivers,
flushes, afire, suddenly tender,
suddenly naked, stung with nettles,

....

The sodden fields stretch into a soft distance.
Those rigid curves of cow parsley:
when I was a child, we called it mother's die.

The Boy as a Fish

When a boy is a fish,
he spins with delight,
his feet slide through liquid air
soft spurts of pleasure blossom on his young skin.
Above, the paper dragon stretches and loops in fresh space.

The sun makes the air thick gold milk.
The leaves by the palace
turn slowly, fall
on a golden boy free as a fish
in a current of fresh oxygen.

Yet the boy is sharp-eyed, wary.
He won't stay: he's been caught before,
little hooks, little twists of
guilt, of duty. He trembles,
jewelled fish in bright enamel.

He's been gulled before,
torn open, entrails in the wind.
The dragon drifts through storm, through grey, gushing water.
Above the smoking palace the sky is endless, endless.
But ah! the fish boy flicks fast away.

Words to Remember

for Ayshe S

Like
>	*village*
>	*fields*
>	*tanks*
>	*dragged*
>	*friend*
>	*girl friend*
>	*tank*

Like
>	*gendarme*
>	*many*
>	*police station*
>	*many*
>	*rape*
>	*many*
>	*rape*

Like
>	*barrister*
>	*appeal*
>	*interpreter*
>	*court*

Always matter of fact.

She knew the other words.
>	Like *husband*.
>	Like *houses*.
>	Like *fire*.
>	Like *uniform*.
>	Like *frightened*.

Like *too sad*. Like *tears*.
Like *I'm sorry, I'm sorry*.
Like *my people, my country*.

After

After what happened,
after the lost days   weeks   months
the arm hangs loose,
hand like plastic.

Look first at the hand,
for the hand is beautiful:
smooth nails, the skin smooth,
the miraculous jointure of the fingers,
the soft unresisting palm.

Or the feet. Beautiful too.
Or the rippling vertebrae of the arched back.
The body as art.

But this is not art.
This is not sculpture.
This is not a picture.

A sculpture inhabits time by asking
what happened before:
this is the end point,
this *thing* is not about to move.

And though this is not sculpture
(sculpture makes no sound)
it must ask the same question.
There will be no after now.
There is only before.

The falling shape of the buttocks,
the hinge of the twisted back,
the arms still strained,
feet roped together.

This is what is left now,
after things have happened.

After the fierce night and the dark places
the crowded streets and the shouting crowds,
After the despairing tenderness of lips,
of eyes, of skin on skin, of hands.

This is what is left
after things have happened.

The headless torso hangs.
Broken.
In the low light of dawn
its slack flesh rendered bronze.

Making a Life

First, how do you make a room?
The setting is important.
A sofa, a table, a chair, a light.
That is enough, more than enough.

A mat may do at a pinch.
Flowers are not necessary.
Fruit is not necessary.
Music however... possibly essential...
but you may try to live without it.

Now you can summon a small place of love –
or its underbelly, rotten with longing
for something made up or gone away.
Its cockroach, a shadow in the dust behind the sofa, under the table.
That mat must be shaken in the cold outside.
That too is a kind of life.

For a life you need an outside,
one that threatens to come in.
That will come in.
That will break this small space.

It may be an outside of tremulous, insistent, darkening hunger,
of improbable need, or desire, of fury.
It will not sit quietly in the small space:
a foot smashes small fingers, a mouth bites at empty air,
a nose is broken to jelly, salt poured and pouring into open wounds.

The small space is in pieces now.
Yet it is a kind of life.

You need a bed too, of course, I had forgotten that –
if only a put up bed off-stage –
and somewhere to hide things.
A mat will do. At a pinch, a cardboard box
can shelter the past in a dark core of tenderness.
Then there is enough, more than enough.

You have a warm small space, an inside to which
an outside may decide to bring flowers,
the flavour of apples,
the creaking sound of a cricket:
humming busyness in a honey glow.

But it is a difficult task.
The actors remain a problem.
They interrupt the flow.
Every moment they clamour for excitement,
trying to move in and out of the small space with grace.

Seated on the sofa, at the table, their eyes, their hair, shown to advantage,
they open their well-formed lips, and they sing. Brightly.
They inhabit the set importantly and, being alive,
they never sit still.

But it is not about them,
they are only the actors.

It is about making a small space where there was nothing,
about an interchange between the outside and the in,
and then a slight silvering of the vacant air.

Crocodiles

Now why should I tell you about this then?
Nothing to me. Why should I care?
I don't get flustered easily.
I like to be quiet, still.

It was getting a bit dark. Best time.
I always slow down in the evenings but that just means
I can watch, see what's going on.
Never let your defences down – that's how to keep smiling.

When he came down the road I knew I had him.
Big bastard. Thought he could get away with it.
Wanker. Cos he's big and throws it about
and I'm quiet, like to lie low like,
he thought I was some push over.
But I was waiting. O yes...

No-one really talks these days so
I reckoned that'd work in my favour.
No-one going to come running,
why should they – out for yourself round here and
if someone can't take it, well, they got it coming.
So I was just there. Waiting,
skin prickling all over but cool like, very cool.

He didn't notice me, I was in the shadows.
I could hear him on his mobile, laughing.
I thought the boot's on the other mate
and stuck my foot out and he went over.

Mobile fell, must have twisted something,
pig gave a surprised grunt, couldn't seem to get up.
I stood there watching him for a bit. Whistled.
I knew I'd got him where I wanted. Laughed.
Well, I pocketed the mobile for a start and swung over.

You want a good kicking eh, I said,
looked him up and down thinking about his weak points –
everywhere of course, big fleshy guy like him.
Funny like an appetite the way it gets you.
A thrill. You almost feel him squeal.

I smiled, showing my teeth, and winked.
He didn't get it of course, like he thought
this wasn't happening. So I gave him a little nip.
Introduction to reality. Starters to get your taste buds going.
Exciting. Very exciting.
you get the taste of it and you feel you just can't stop.

And wouldn't you like to know what happened?
Nice and tidy. Wouldn't you just?
Low life that's what he was, deserved everything.
Plenty more scum.
Thought he was a big fish but he was just a laugh.
Needed a bit of respect.

But like I said why should I tell you about this?
I like to be cool, still. Quiet. Yes quiet.

Not I

A black hole, empty air and a mouth speaking.
It goes on. And on.
Disembodied, feverish.
It shrieks of birth, abandonment, a waste of days,
and of a spring moment:
an old woman picking cowslips in the sunny meadow,
of falling and the soft and sudden, lovely, numbing dark.

The mouth shrieks, lit up, a terrible instrument,
The voice repeats a story, repeats it,
insists it is the story of someone else,
of someone else, of someone else.

There is nothing to be seen,
there is nothing but empty air,
we hallucinate misshapen horrors hanging above us
or see ourselves.

There is nothing in the vacuum
except us, except
the shrill mechanical voice that is us,
the hot red mouth, the white teeth on the edge of tearing an
uncontrollable tongue that writhes, endlessly, in frenzy.
Fades in frenzy as the dark slides over.
The echo: this is not, this is not
about me.

The Orange Juice Story

I hate this uniform,
nylon, orange, hot, sticky and
my make-up streaks under my eyes.

The baby wouldn't settle last night,
and Sophia cried with the heat.
Juan shouted I was no good,

told me he'd be waiting when I got back.
Sophia heard and stopped crying –
she's sharp for three.

The baby was sick on the bed again.
The third time this week. I need a doctor but
my money disappears down Juan's throat.

You see my hands are out of control,
that's how it happened.
I've done it hundreds of times, no trouble,

but this time I turned too quickly,
put the plastic cup under the spout,
and knocked it flying.

When I was a child the smell of oranges,
warm and glowing in the tree outside my house
just beautiful. Before everything.

Now I can't do anything properly.
Six hours before I go home.
Miriam in the kitchen screaming I'll have to pay.

I tried to look good this morning
because inside I'm dizzy
with all the things that go wrong.

My hands sticky with juice, thick sticky pulp
on my face, on the floor, in my shoes, in my bra.
That woman just shrugged and waited. Smiled.

I wanted to hit her. I heard the other one say
'no use crying over split orange juice'.
And just what would she know?

After a While

for Najma and Abdullah

After a while the child got used to it,
he played in the corridors
and never asked for his father.
Though sometimes, dreaming in the night,
he shouted the forgotten name.
And when the phone rang asked, over and over
Who is that, mama, who is that?

But really he had forgotten.
He was happy in the clean small room,
he played happily.

Sometimes now he wet the bed:
over excitement.
No doubt.

He had forgotten his nursery,
the names of the children crowding his dream lives,
waving their hands excitedly.
He had forgotten everything:
forgotten the stairs to the flat,
the old man from the next door room
who gave him chocolate,
had forgotten the soft white fur
of the toy cat that ate the dinosaurs
that lived in the broken fridge,
forgotten the woman in the shop across the road
who sold newspapers and smiled at him.
He had forgotten the road outside and the beach
where his father went running in the morning.

He was adaptable.
This was now:
the small room,
the grown-ups shuffling round,
whispering in corners.

He had forgotten his father.
He played as his mother cried.
It was all the same to him.
He was only a child with a bright face,
bright eyes and screaming laughter.

After the shouting at the airport
he had forgotten his father
who had gone to the toilet
and never come back.

And you say

you will write no more poems.
How can my tenderness utter itself without verses
that set your heartbeats to a music shimmering with ardour?
Truth reveals itself in melodies
whose harmonies frame passion in pure intensity.

Do my letters prove that you are my soul, my heart, my being?
that in your presence I discover myself?
The clouds rain warm love,
the flood spills over my words and writings:
your love gifts my life with the happiness of dream.

It is enough that you lie at the core of my soul:
a tide breaching my deepest boundaries,
a star drawing my shape to fuller existence.
Your love is greater than these words, stronger than me:
you are the dawn of my every Eid morning.

Translated with the author from the Arabic of Amani Omer Bakhiet

لن اكتُبَكِ بعد الآن قصيده
و هل يعبّركَ الشوقُ دونَ سطورٍ
تعزفُ نبضاً... تسطعُ بوحاً
راية صدقٍ... تصدحُ حينا
لحناً صاغ الوجد معاني فريده

و هل تُنبئنكَ حروفي انكَ روحي
قلبي و ذاتي.. تهبّ ثباتي
سّحباً تُمطرٌ عشقاً دافئ
فيض فاق حدودَ الوصفِ.. و الكلماتِ
حُلماً اهدي العمر ليالي سعيده

و يكفي أنك بين ضلوعي
مدٌّ يعبّر عُمقَ حدودي
رمزٌ حددَ شكلَ وجودي
فجرٌ حطمَ طوقَ يودي
لِيبقى حبَّك فوقَ الكَلمةِ اقوي مني
و تَبقى لكل صباح طلة عِيده

I Journey Towards You

I journey towards you
joining the fastest caravan,
seeking to overtake time.

I journey towards you
I will give you new worlds
with the recovery of love, the loss of suffering.

I journey towards you.
Miracles will be inspired by your love,
marvellous songs will choose
the wide space of your breast to be their home.

I journey towards you.
to be close to you,
to be cradled by wings in the morning of love,
to be sheltered in the light of your dawn.

I journey towards you.
The passionate beaches
ache to touch the clouds.
They crave the waters of your ocean.

I journey towards you.
I journey towards you.

Translated with the author from the Arabic of Amani Omer Bakhiet

اليك ارتحل
قوافلا تسارع الخطي
تسابق الزمن

اليك ارتحل
عوالماً لأجلك
تعانق الهوي تفارق الشجن

اليك ارتحل
روائعاً بحبك
توقع الغناء
تصطفي رحاب صدرك

اليك ارتحل
جوانحاً لقربك
تداعب الصباح
تحتمي بنور صدرك

اليك ارتحل
سواحلاً مشوقه
تغازل السحاب
تشتهي مياه بحرك

اليك ارتحل
اليك ارتحل

Acknowledgements

Acknowledgements are due to the following magazines and anthologies where some of these poems first appeared: *Agenda, Fragments from the Dark, New Welsh Review, New Writing, Orbis, Planet, Poetry Wales, Soft Touch* and *The London Magazine.*